Hazel Scott
A Woman, a Piano, and a Commitment to Justice

Hazel Scott
A Woman, a Piano, and a Commitment to Justice

by Susan Engle

illustrated by Luthando Mazibuko

BELLWOOD
PRESS®
WILMETTE, ILLINOIS

401 Greenleaf Ave, Wilmette, Illinois 60091
Copyright © 2021 by the National Spiritual Assembly
of the Bahá'ís of the United States
All rights reserved. Published 2021
Printed in the United States of America ∞

24   23   22   21   4   3   2   1

**Library of Congress Cataloging in Publication
Control Number: 2021903890**

Cover and book design by Patrick Falso
Illustrations by Luthando Mazibuko

Contents

Acknowledgments

When looking at the story of Hazel Scott's life, it is easy to see faith written all over it—faith in God, faith in herself, and faith in her talents. Faith, to me, is the opposite of fear, and Hazel clearly showed faith in her fearless pursuit of justice, both for herself and for all African Americans. I hope you can feel the inspiration I felt as I read about the journey of her life and wrote this biography.

I am forever grateful to my daughters, Bahiyyih Baker and Layli Phillips, and to Bonnie Taylor for having faith in me as an author who would be able to write books for readers like you. There is also a quiet guardian angel who assisted me in my writing and who does not wish to be acknowledged here. She helped me describe Hazel's life by adding insights from her own. What would we do without our friends?

May you, dear reader, always read history with an eye for truth. May you be inspired by this story, and by the stories of all heroes, to become your truest, most fearless self.

Introduction

The toddler started howling. Her mother looked over her shoulder to see what was bothering her daughter. This was the third time during the lesson with her piano student that the little child had started screaming. True, the new student did keep hitting the wrong notes, but it just did not seem possible that her two-year-old could be so sensitive to clinkers. When the student played all the right notes, however, her daughter became quiet, turned around, and pretended to play the piano on the front of the seat of her little chair.

Yes, her mother knew her daughter was bright in many ways, and she surrounded her with music. The child's father, however, was much more interested in developing her intellectual curiosity. He had become a teacher because he loved the field of education. He had a gift for learning languages, including various dialects of Chinese, and his daughter showed the same talent for learning a variety of languages as she grew older.

Her father also wanted her to understand the burden that black people shouldered, especially those who were living in the Caribbean, where Hazel was born, and in the United States, where the family members moved a few years later. So when his daughter was four years old, he began to take her, without her mother's knowledge, to large meetings organized by a charismatic man named Marcus Garvey.[1]

The meetings Mr. Garvey held at the Universal Negro Improvement Association in Harlem were filled with pageantry and a sense of empowerment for black people. Black Cross Nurses—women who helped provide health services to the black community—were standing in their crisp, white uniforms in a dignified row at the front of the room.[2] Wearing gold braids, medals, and uniforms designed only for the Association, men stood at attention. The air was filled with a sense of black dignity and pride.

At these meetings, African Americans could gather and celebrate the contributions they had made to the country for

over two hundred years, even though these contributions were unappreciated by white people.[3] Under the suffocating burden of slavery, black people had been forced to perform back-breaking labor, with no pay, to contribute to the thriving economy of the Southern states. Black people had also

been compelled to build homes and plantations in the South, as well as the White House and the U.S. Capitol in Washington, D.C. Additionally, black men and women had given their lives during the Civil War, the Spanish-American War, and the First World War, yet they had come home to face continued rejection and prejudice from the majority of their fellow white soldiers and nurses and the majority of white Americans, including white representatives in federal, state, and local governments.[4]

Mr. Garvey's message of "black is beautiful" spoke to the father and his child. His motto "One God, One Aim, One

Destiny" also made perfect sense, and the little girl would remember Mr. Garvey's message of the potential black people possessed, no matter how many white people showed her over the years that *they* did not accept this.[5] She could and did believe in these values.

Whenever the child returned from this kind of a field trip with her father, she would say nothing to her mother, who always thought that her daughter and husband had been to the Bronx Zoo or had taken a stroll through the park. If her mother had ever found out about these trips to listen to Mr. Garvey, she would have put a stop to them. Her mother believed that it was no use burdening the little girl with something she could not do anything about at such a young age. There was no sense, she reasoned, in letting her daughter know how difficult things could be for black people. But her daughter was beginning to understand much about the ever-present oppression of her people and the beauty of standing up for one's rights.

The little girl's family surrounded her with high expectations for a good life. After all, she was the only one of her parents' seven children to live more than a few months after birth. Somehow, she felt as if she needed to be the smartest and most accomplished person in the world to make up for being the only surviving child, and she quickly learned how to use both her musical talent and her quick mind. She was determined to make her dreams come true, and she grew to be strong and self-assured. Her responsibility to her family and her people always remained at the forefront of her mind and heart.

Later, a music critic and producer wrote about her exceptional musical talent. He also described her strong personality, both on stage and in life. He wrote, "The bright-eyed jubilance with which she performed could freeze in an instant. Nobody who ever saw her will forget her habit of stopping suddenly, transfixing any noisemaker with an icy glare and waiting for total silence before she resumed. Some thought her arrogant; others knew that she simply demanded respect."[6]

1 / Music Inside, Music Outside

Beautiful Trinidad is a land of pure, blue skies; deep, blue-green ocean waters; bright butterflies; and tiny birds. When the Arawak Indians were the main residents long ago, they named it "Land of the Hummingbird."[7] Eighteen different species of hummingbirds live on the island, which is hot and humid for half of the year and hot and dry for the other half.

On June 11, 1920, a child was born, in the city of Port of Spain, to Alma Long

Scott and R. Thomas Scott during the rainy season. They named her Hazel Dorothy, and she was a big, healthy, bouncing baby girl weighing twelve pounds. Her parents were thrilled and hopeful that this baby, unlike the children born before her, might live and grow into a healthy adult woman.

From the beginning, Hazel's life was filled with music. Her mother, Alma, wanted nothing more than to be a concert pianist. Though Alma worked hard outside the home and took odd jobs to support the family, she made sure that she had time to practice the piano. She honed her already considerable ability to play scales and to learn long pieces of music.

What she did not know, even after all her years of practice, was that she had weak wrists that could not withstand the stress of a performance of classical piano pieces.[8] When she was given the opportunity to give a solo concert in Trinidad, the length of the program caused Alma's wrists so much pain that she could not finish playing. She was surprised and sad to discover this, and she tried for some time to strengthen her wrists with exercises and medical help. She gave up on the idea of a career performing classical music, but she continued to play at home. Music was the one thing in life that she loved above all else, so she also began to give piano lessons. As a child, little Hazel took in the beautiful piano pieces her mother played, along with the voice of her grandmother, Margaret, who would sing her to sleep for her afternoon nap.

One day, while singing a hymn, Margaret fell asleep instead of Hazel, who was two and a half years old at the time. The toddler went to the piano, and, using both of her hands, began to play the hymn by ear.

The music woke Margaret, who, thinking that a stranger had come inside the house, called out, "Who's there?"

She heard a little voice answer, "Me."[9]

Of course, it was Hazel.[10]

Margaret ran to the street and called out for neighbors to come. When they walked into the house, no one could believe what they were seeing and hearing. Such a little child, playing without any instruction! It was then that Alma knew that her daughter was going to be the major piano player in the family, and she did all that she could to teach Hazel everything she knew.

When the piano lessons started, Alma discovered other things about her daughter. Hazel had perfect pitch, and she did not mind working hard to please her mother. Hazel continued to play by ear, and her playing reflected the rhythms and melodies of the music—calypso—that surrounded her outside in the streets of Trinidad.

She played so well that she began to perform at small get-togethers. Her mother would dress her up in beautiful little silk and satin dresses and put ribbons and bows in her hair. The people listening would dance, clap, and encourage Hazel while enjoying the music. These experiences were inspiring for the child, and Hazel fell in love with playing for an audience.

After Hazel's younger brother—the family's seventh and last child—died, her parents began to drift apart. Hazel's father, who was "weary of home life," spent less and less time with Alma and Hazel.[11] He longed to teach at an African-American university in the United States, so he left Trinidad for good. Not too long afterward, Alma and Margaret also became eager to move to the United States and take Hazel with them. They had heard that they could earn far better wages in New York City than they could in Port of Spain. Alma's sister, Lilla, already lived there, so they would have a place to stay until they could afford a house of their own.

Margaret left Trinidad first to earn enough money to buy tickets for her daughter and granddaughter to join the family in New York. By Hazel's fourth birthday—June 11, 1924—Hazel and Alma were traveling aboard a ship called the *Maraval*.[12] They were headed for a new life in a new city where Alma hoped they would have enough income to support

Hazel's talent. As far as Alma was concerned, Hazel was destined for a professional musical career.

2 / A New Home in Harlem

Hazel loved the voyage by ship to the United States! While her mother, who suffered constantly from seasickness, would often take naps in their cabin, Hazel did not want to sit still. She soon sneaked out of their cabin to explore.

Despite being so young, Hazel was fearless, and she was hoping she could find a piano somewhere on the ship. She spoke to a few fellow passengers who were out walking on the decks, but they could not help her. Then she ran into the captain.

Immediately, she told him that she was four years old, that it was her birthday, and she could play the piano. Years later, she remembered that he was "enormously amused and set about making me prove my claim."[13]

He led her to the piano on board, and Hazel played for the people who gathered around. As usual, she enjoyed performing. What better way to have a birthday party? When Alma woke up, she saw that Hazel was missing and began searching for her daughter. She was not surprised to find her sitting at a piano and entertaining a crowd of people. Alma tried to encourage Hazel to return to their room, but she was completely unsuccessful. Hazel was in her element, and she was determined to stay there.[14] As obedient and caring as Hazel wanted to be, the urge to play the piano was unstoppable for her.

When the *Maraval* docked in New York City, Hazel and Alma were astonished by their new surroundings. Gone were the palm trees, the royal blue skies, and the calypso music on the street. Here in the section of New York called Harlem, Hazel and Alma saw brown buildings, crowded streets, bright signs, and bits of sky visible between towering buildings.

The one thing that was familiar to Hazel and Alma were the brown and black faces they saw at every turn. These families, migrating from the southern United States and from places like Trinidad, were replacing the white families who had lived here for decades. New York City, like other northern and western cities in the United States, was a place that offered jobs with

good pay for people who could earn very little elsewhere, particularly in the rural south.[15]

Harlem was also filled with a new, exciting sound and feel. Books, poems, dance, and music created by black people were fast becoming popular, and this period would later become known as the Harlem Renaissance. Although it was not calypso, the music floating out of windows and doors had the energetic sounds of horns and drums, big bands and jazz.

After she and her mother arrived at her aunt's brownstone in Harlem, Hazel was content to see so many family members. The rooms were filled with Hazel's cousins, uncles, and aunts, along with friends who had also traveled to New York from Trinidad.

Hazel's father would stop in every now and then to take her someplace that he felt was important for her education, but Thomas never stayed long afterward. Hazel's grandmother, who still sang hymns and who continued to work many hours outside the home, insisted that her daughters cook delicious homemade meals for the family, even if she could not be there to supervise. They would prepare traditional dishes from Trinidad, and she would make sure lots of spice was included, along with peppers, garlic, curry, coconut milk, lime, and brown sugar. Rice, green plantains, stewed chicken, okra, pumpkin, and onions were often on the table as well, and the house would be filled with the familiar smells of Hazel's grandmother's preferred foods that were cooking and baking in the oven. And on Sundays—what a feast! Hazel remembers, "There was wonderful food for Communion breakfast. Rich chocolate from Trinidad, homemade buttered bread, baked ham studded with cloves. I was glad to be alive."[16]

Life was not easy for Hazel, though. During the week, when everyone else in the house went to work, Hazel was left alone with her Aunt Lilla. Although they were family, her aunt treated the people in the house—especially Hazel and her mother—as if they were intruders. She spoke to Hazel coldly and trained the little girl to run all of her errands for her. By the time Hazel was five, she became the person who paid the bills. When Lilla left the house, Hazel gave cash to whoever came to collect money for insurance, gas, or electricity.

The whole neighborhood marveled that little Hazel had been given this responsibility when she was on her own at home. Unfortunately, the story of a little girl with a lot of cash became so well-known that, one day, some young men broke into the house through a downstairs window. They told Hazel to give them all of her aunt's money, but Hazel would not give them anything, so the "white ruffians" began to beat her.[17]

Hazel started screaming! Neighbors heard her and called the police for help. With sirens blaring, cars filled with policemen drove up, and the officers stayed until the adults started to return home. Lilla had hysterics when she saw the house full of policemen, as she felt that a proper family home simply should not be the scene of a crime! When Hazel's mother arrived from work, she wept when she saw her daughter, bruised and bleeding. After Alma was told that Hazel had been paying the bills for Lilla, Alma fainted, as she had no idea Hazel had been left on her own with this responsibility.[18]

The young men did not return to hurt Hazel again. Hazel's family had tried to protect her from the racial tension in Harlem by not talking about it with her. However, it was impossible to hide the fact that some white people felt as if they were being forced out of Harlem by incoming black residents. These white people often retaliated against black families with violence, and even a five-year-old black child was not always safe.

Hazel was very much aware from her experience that ignoring the problem of racism would not make it go away. Because she already knew how to read, she carefully studied newspaper articles about injustices being committed against black people. When her mother found out about her young daughter's reading habits, she would not let Hazel read the papers at home. But since she was still running errands for Aunt Lilla, Hazel would stop to read the newspaper at the newsstand long before she walked in the door of her aunt's brownstone.[19]

Alma knew that, under her fearless exterior, Hazel was a sensitive, dreamy little girl who loved making up games and playing piano. She also knew Hazel was slowly being molded by her experiences to become tough and resilient—qualities that would serve her well on the city's streets. However, the most important thing that Alma knew about Hazel was that what she loved with all her heart was sharing her musical talent with people.

After her daughter had been beaten, Alma redoubled her efforts to give Hazel opportunities to perform.

3 / Piano, Piano, Piano

Now piano lessons began in earnest. Alma taught Hazel how to play scales, how to place her fingers on the keys correctly, and how to sightread. Though Hazel sometimes rebelled and started playing calypso in the middle of practice, her mother overlooked her rebelliousness. She would repeat to her daughter as she played, "Face forward, head up, shoulders relaxed, flat back, hands spread gracefully over the keys."[20] Soon, Hazel knew classical pieces that were perfect for being played in churches. She had memorized "Jesu, Joy of Man's Desiring" by Johann Sebastian Bach and "Ave Maria" by Charles Gounod. As Hazel's training progressed, Alma made sure she had an audience, and on Sundays, Hazel would play at church congregations all over Harlem.[21]

Alma was also searching for competitions and auditions for her five-year-old daughter, and Hazel played her first professional recital at Town Hall in Manhattan in 1925.[22] She had just begun elementary school in Harlem, and word of her success soon reached the students and parents. Though Hazel became popular for her talent, she was often invited—solely for her playing ability—to her classmates' birthday parties. As a result, the children at these parties would often ignore her until the mother or father of the birthday child asked her to play. Then the boys and parents in the room would draw close and listen attentively to her polished piano pieces, and when she finished playing, they would enthusiastically applaud. The girls at the party, however, reacted differently. They often withdrew to a different part of the room and, jealous of the attention she received, would whisper things to her after her performances such as, "We only invited you so that you could play the piano."[23]

As a result, Hazel never doubted her talent, but she often questioned everything else about herself, including her looks. She thought she looked mousey, she did not like her hair, and she regretted having a full bottom lip. She said, "Teased about it, I caught it in my teeth and went around holding it that way."[24] She did not develop close friendships with people her age, and she continued to spend her free time at home alone. There she would read and write in her diary and let her imagination roam.

Only three years after her first recital, Alma walked through the doors of Juilliard School with Hazel to arrange an audition.

This excellent school for the performing arts promised its students: "At Juilliard you will learn to interpret music of any period—to nurture it, refine it, give it life, and make it your own."[25] Though only students who were sixteen or older were admitted at the time, Alma was able to convince someone at the school to hear her eight-year-old daughter.

Hazel was taken to a practice room where Professor Oscar Wagner settled in to listen to her play a piece by Rachmaninoff titled "Prelude in C Sharp Minor." Hazel's hands were not large enough to play all the octaves that the composer had written. Instead, she played notes that were sixth chords because she liked the way they sounded, and because she could.

While she performed, the head of the school, Frank Damrosch, was passing in the hall and heard the substituted notes. Quite unhappy, he yelled out, "Who is that paraphrasing Rachmaninoff?" When he saw it was little Hazel, he stopped, shocked to see a little girl. "I was only reaching the closest thing that it sounded like," Hazel wrote later about her explanation to Mr. Damrosch, "not even knowing what a sixth was . . ." Professor Wagner was impressed by her ingenuity. After she had finished, he said in a low voice, "I am in the presence of genius."[26]

The students at Juilliard were mostly white males, but Professor Wagner took her on as a private pupil. He was instrumental in giving Hazel a strong sense of her ability as a pianist.[27] They worked together for about ten years, until the professor became too ill to teach.

Now that Hazel was in school, she was no longer running so many errands for her aunt. She would go to public school in Harlem, then downtown to Juilliard for hours of lessons. After that, Hazel headed home for dinner, chores, homework, and more piano practice.

She also began to challenge her teachers during these years, as she was learning how to speak up when she saw injustice. Sometimes, she went beyond speaking up and was just plain rude. Talking back to teachers was not appreciated in either the school, the principal's office, or at home. Whenever her mother scolded her for these incidents, Hazel returned to her bedroom refuge and her diary, where she would continue to make up a life with happy endings.[28]

4 / The First Big Break

Ever since their move to New York from Trinidad, Hazel's mother and grandmother had wanted a home of their own. Finally, Alma and Margaret had enough money to put a down payment on a brownstone just a block away from Aunt Lilla's.[29] Even with the economic problems in the United States that arrived with the stock market crash in 1929, the women of the household were determined to make things work for them in Harlem.

First, Alma opened a tailoring shop in the lower floor of the house. When washing, ironing, and even dying clothes did not pay well, she opened a Chinese restaurant! Alma was a good cook, and for a while, the restaurant was successful. Eventually, however, the restaurant was robbed. After the third robbery, Alma became discouraged and closed it.[30] What she really wanted to do was to return to her first love—music.

All-black female swing bands had started to become popular, so Alma rented a saxophone and began to teach herself how to play. She not only had to learn a new instrument, she had to learn a new style of music. In jazz—unlike classical music—the notes are sometimes improvised and not always written down. She practiced for months while her neighbors and family laughed at her. Hazel, on the other hand, always spoke up to defend her mother. Her outspokenness was fast becoming a permanent part of her personality. She later wrote, "The neighbors were always eager to find out what my poor mother was up to. A woman without a man to support her, she constantly intrigued men and women alike with her resourcefulness."[31] Alma cared nothing about her neighbors' opinions. She was interested not only in music, but in survival. If playing the saxophone would pay the bills, so be it.

Finally, Alma was ready to audition to play saxophone in a band. She had taught herself well and landed one gig after another. She often traveled and saved money to send home to pay the mortgage.[32] Hazel had her grandmother to look after her, so Alma felt that she could travel without worrying about her daughter. Whenever she did come home, the brownstone became a place where well-known jazz musicians she had met on the road would drop by to play some tunes.[33]

It was during these informal jam sessions that Hazel met people who influenced her playing—and her life—forever after. Fats Waller, Art Tatum, and Billie Holiday were only a few of the new faces who became like family to her. In Billie, Hazel felt as if she had suddenly acquired a big sister. Art Tatum became "Papa Daddy" since Hazel's father was seldom in her life.[34]

Whenever Thomas Scott did visit, he let Hazel know that he did not want her to be a performer, and Hazel, of course, did not share her father's view at all. She would later say, "He took me to see *The Merchant of Venice* because he wanted me to be a lawyer. And I came out and announced that I was going to be an actress. I saw the expression on his face. He hated the thought of my being involved with anything to do with performing, showing yourself to the public."[35]

Papa Daddy, on the other hand, understood her love for playing the piano. Because she had an excellent ear and nimble fingers, Hazel could learn the key changes and flourishes that distinguished Mr. Tatum's style of piano from other jazz pianists. He taught her how to make piano music swing, along with his version of "Tea for Two" that she would use later in her own career.[36]

Hazel was in an all-girl middle school in Harlem by the time she was eleven years old. Gone was the rebelliousness—some would call it rudeness—of her grade school years. She now approached her schoolwork seriously, with the same discipline that she brought to her studies at Juilliard with Professor Wagner. Her gift for languages emerged, and she quickly began learning French, German, and Spanish. She would also read newspapers in various languages that she could find easily in the city.

Hazel surprised her mother one night by popping onstage to sing at the Apollo Theater when Alma was playing there with an all-women band called the Harlem Harlicans. "I was supposed to be in bed,"

Hazel later wrote. "[Mother] later said to me, 'You're running around here singing pop tunes. Well, if you like that sort of thing . . . here's how it should sound.' And mother went and played an Ethel Waters record for me."[37]

Alma found more piano concerts for her daughter, and by the time Hazel was

thirteen, she was being booked as "Little Miss Hazel Scott—Child Wonder Pianist."[38] During this time, Hazel also took on a full-time job playing piano accompaniment for ballet and modern dance classes. Sometimes, she even slipped into a dance class herself at Mabel Laws Horsey's Dance Studio.

Billie Holiday regularly showed up at the brownstone to hang out in the kitchen with Alma. If Alma occasionally became distracted with her own career playing saxophone, Billie would bug her about opportunities *she* could arrange for Hazel. One such audition took place with a well-known composer and bandleader named

Noble Sissle. Thirteen-year-old Hazel's job during the tryout was to accompany a young singer and to calmly and expertly make all the musical changes Mr. Sissle called out while she was playing piano. This singer would, in a few years, work with Hazel again. Her name was Lena Horne.[39]

When Hazel was fourteen, she began to find her grandmother's supervision at home difficult to bear. Though Margaret was never cruel or particularly unkind to her, Hazel felt no warmth in their daily interactions. Alma was away from home often, and her career had blossomed from gigs with a band of all-black women led by trumpeter Louis Armstrong's wife, Lil, to playing with an all-male band of black musicians, led by Chick Webb, at the Savoy Ballroom. Since Alma was the only female player with Chick Webb's band—an unusual accomplishment in the 1930s—she sometimes had to deal with sexist comments about a female playing saxophone. It was not unusual for someone to come up to the bandstand and say, "Lady, you play that thing just like a man." Whenever she heard a statement like this, Alma would sometimes reply, "Mister, you carry your children just like a lady."[40]

Eventually, Alma decided that she was ready to start her own band so she could be in control of her schedule, and Alma Long Scott's American Creolians was born. Hazel was eager to get away from her grandmother's cold behavior. "I . . . had badgered my mother into allowing me to play in her orchestra," she later wrote. "I told her very calmly that 'I cannot stay home with people who aren't in the business . . .' I said if she didn't let me play in the orchestra I would become a juvenile delinquent. She was upset—she wanted me to play the classics—but she relented."[41]

Up to this time, Hazel had always thought that she was not very good-looking. But now, boys were beginning to pay attention to her. She wrote, "I had suddenly become a swan."[42] Though Hazel was a professional when it came to the piano, she had started to draw a lot of attention to herself by flirting with the audience during her gigs with the Creolians. It bothered the other women in the orchestra so much that Alma decided to find a way to get her out.

Alma managed to find Hazel a spot on the same stage as the Count Basie Orchestra, one of the most popular bands in the 1930s and 40s.[43] Maybe she was able to accomplish this because William Basie, nicknamed "Count" because he was considered jazz "royalty," admired

Alma's friends Fats Waller and Billie Holiday. Whatever the reason, Hazel's playing between Count Basie's sets became a big break for her career.

"There I stood in the wings," Hazel remembered, "staring round-eyed at the beautiful young man out on the stage playing incredible jazz and [I] began to shake. My teeth all but chattered and I was ready to call it a life right then and there!" As the band began one of their most popular tunes, "One O'Clock Jump," and the audience drew close to the stage, the Count looked at her and winked.[44] When he had finished his part of the program, he adjusted the microphone for Hazel. She gathered the courage to step out onstage and wowed the crowd with her characteristic classical and boogie-woogie musical mix. By the time she had finished, she was a "huge hit" with the audience packed in at the Roseland Ballroom.[45]

All Hazel's training had led her to this moment, and she had proven herself capable and ready for the spotlight. She began to view her career with a seriousness that, until now, had been missing. She was filled with "the desire to reach an audience," Hazel wrote, "[and] to communicate a beauty that ha[d] been entrusted to [my] care . . ."[46]

5 / Steps to Fame and Fortune

The economic depression that was creeping up on the country was affecting Alma's orchestra. It was becoming expensive to pay all the musicians for their work and transport them to and from their gigs at home and on the road. As a result, Alma was expecting Hazel's work to bring in more income for the family now. After all, Hazel was fifteen years old, with exceptional training and experience for such a young person.

Hazel's father died during this time. His death was not a financial blow, as her father had never really helped the family with finances. Hazel had known for a long time that he had not approved of her career in show business. He had been the parent who had wanted her to devote her life to study and to standing up for her people instead of standing in the spotlight.[47] Hazel, however, was determined to do both.

The depression brought hard times to Harlem. People lost jobs. They felt wronged and desperate. Money was scarce, children were starving, and crime was a regular occurrence. Alma was nervous about Hazel traveling to and from gigs, so she asked Billie Holiday and other friends to keep an eye out for her.[48] Being young and carefree, however, Hazel wanted to appear as if she were an adult with no supervision needed.

One night, Billie was a few feet away when she overheard Hazel tell a fellow musician that she was eighteen years old, though she was only fifteen at the time. As soon as the words had left her mouth, Hazel heard a yell. She saw Billie head her way, looking and sounding fierce. Hazel fled down the street to the subway ahead of Billie, but she finally stopped to face her pursuer. "You're not going to tell my mother, are you?" she asked Billie. "Tell her?" was Billie's reply. "I'm going to sit there and watch her knock you down!"[49]

Protecting Hazel from fellow musicians who could take advantage of her was one thing. Protecting Hazel from the judgement of her mother's displeasure, however, was not Billie's concern. How Alma reacted to this episode is not known; regardless, Hazel's life and career continued to sail along smoothly.

In addition to being a superb pianist, Hazel had become quite an accomplished singer ever since she had surprised her mother by singing at the Apollo Theater when she was eleven years old. One of her other protector friends, Ken Harrison, found out about an audition for a radio station called WOR, The Voice of New York. Nervous and concerned for her, Ken began to tell her what to do and what to say at the audition. When Hazel had heard enough, she said to him, "Ken! Kindly do not tell me how to conduct business! We will go to the audition and I will play and sing, as I have been doing for eleven years!"[50] When the audition was over, she had beaten out hundreds of competitors, and she had won a six-month contract with WOR. Additionally, at the age of fifteen, she had also been given the freedom to choose the music she would perform!

By now, Hazel's schedule was unrelenting, and she was playing in recitals and in nightclubs during her high school years. Then in 1938, she had to make room for a new opportunity. She was cast in a Broadway musical—*Sing Out the News*—at the Music Box Theater! In the chorus, she sang a solo called "Franklin D. Roosevelt Jones." It was the story of a black child who was filled with hope because of President Roosevelt and his policies in Washington, D.C., that would help the poor and oppressed people of the United States. Audiences and critics loved the way she sang the solo. The producers loved it, too, and they increased her salary from sixty-five to one hundred dollars a week. (One hundred dollars in 1938 would be equivalent to almost $1800 in 2020.[51]) She was handsomely fulfilling her obligation to help support her family.

After her Broadway debut, Hazel began playing piano and singing at the Yacht Club in New York City.[52] Her job was to entertain the audience between the sets of a well-known cabaret singer and pianist, Frances Faye. Miss Faye listened to her perform while she ate her supper. Every time Hazel started a popular song, Miss Faye would send a busboy over to tell Hazel, "You can't do that number. Miss Faye does it in the show." Finally, one evening, Hazel became fed up with Miss Faye's interference. She said to herself, "I know. I'll play the Bach Inventions and I'll syncopate them, really up, up tempo, and see if she does THAT in her show."[53]

Inadvertently, Miss Faye had led Hazel to the moment that would eventually help Hazel become a star. For years to come, audiences listening to Hazel would want to hear her jazz up the classics, and it became her signature style.[54]

Not everyone was thrilled with Hazel's take on much-loved classical pieces, and one of these people was Alma. Hazel wrote, "My mother hated it. She was a purist—[she] liked her jazz straight and her classics straight. She'd just shake her head."[55]

But Papa Daddy loved what she was doing and arranged for her take over for him at the Famous Door, a popular jazz club in Manhattan. Juilliard-trained pianist Dr. Matthew Kennedy, who became the director of the much-praised Fisk Jubilee Singers, thought Hazel's jazzy classics were exceptional. He wrote, "It involved a lot of interpretation. And a special feel for it, a very special talent, which Hazel Scott had."[56]

However, Hazel's increased popularity was coming at a cost. She wrote that all this activity "exacted a frightful toll . . . There were times when I thought that I just couldn't go on."[57] Her days were filled with sleep-deprived hours at high school and endless practice for evening work at major clubs in the city. Then came the extensive rehearsals and performances of a Broadway musical. Perhaps the hardest responsibility added during this year was the creation of the Hazel Scott Band by her friend Ken Harrison. She played and sang with the band—also called Fourteen Men and a Girl—but it was one activity too many for her, and the band did not last long.[58]

Yet somehow, during these exhausting days, Hazel added Yiddish, Italian, and Chinese to the list of languages she learned to read. She still possessed her talent—which had been so valued by her late father—for learning new languages easily. She also succeeded in graduating from high school with honors! However, she was forced to end her valued relationship with her piano teacher, Professor Wagner, when he became ill. He had trained her at Juilliard since she was eight years old, and although her schedule now became lighter, her heart was heavier. In one short year, she had experienced so many victories and trials!

Then, in 1939, Billie Holliday stepped in to change her life a little more. A new club had opened in Harlem called Café Society. Unlike the Cotton Club, where black musicians played for a white audience, this club was based on equality and diversity. There were plenty of black performers, but the audience included people from any and every culture who wanted to come in and hear the vibrant music. It was like no other club in New York City at the time. Hazel said, "I kept expecting something violent to happen when I came out to sing and saw one or two Negroes at a table of white guests or several tables of Negro guests threaded throughout the audience. But there was never an explosion. The waiters never refused to serve anyone, and no guests ever shoved back their chairs and stormed out. . . . Instead, the guests not only remained for dinner and the show, but, white and Negro, they invited the performers to join them at their tables."[59]

One of the performers at Café Society was Billie. Her rendition of a song called "Strange Fruit" was attracting huge crowds. The lyrics provided a powerful description of a lynching in the South. Silence was requested for this song, and people were visibly moved as Billie ended each night with this condemnation of the all-too-present practice of the murdering of black people in the United States. Though Billie was a headliner at Café Society, her time at the nightclub was coming to an end. Before she left, she asked Barney Josephson, the club owner, to bring in Hazel to replace her.

Hazel played, and she stayed. By the time she had been at the nightclub for two years, a second location of Café Society had opened in uptown Manhattan, and she was receiving top billing in the new club. The publicity from the club's opening signaled the start of her national breakthrough as a jazz pianist and singer.[60] Stories about her performances reached popular national publications, such as *Time* and *Collier's* magazines.[61] She was seen with fans such as Eleanor Roosevelt, singer and actor Paul Robeson, Duke Ellington, and many others.[62] Similar to Billie's success at Café Society, Hazel's performances—especially her take on swing-ing the classics—resulted in full houses every night.[63] Soon, she would record her first album, and her music would be played far beyond the limits of New York City. Hazel Scott was fast becoming "one of the most popular artists of her generation."[64]

6 / Hazel in Hollywood

Now Hazel was the major breadwinner in the family, and she was supporting her mother and grandmother in fine style. Her pay at Café Society grew to $1,500 a week, which is equivalent to more than $27,500 today.[65] She was able to buy designer gowns, furs, and jewelry that emphasized her elegant style as a woman and a performer. Her dressing room was "as big as an apartment," and she was only nineteen years old.[66] Most of her life had been spent in the music business, so she was knowledgeable about what she could and could not do on stage. Audiences loved her, and she loved them right back.

Her musical talent went beyond her own playing and improvisation. She was hired by famed saxophonist Coleman Hawkins to arrange music for his band. People were hungry for her particular style, so a few months later, she recorded her first solo album for the Decca record label. It was called *Swinging the Classics: Piano Solos in Swing Style with Drums*. In the first few weeks, it sold thousands of copies—more sales than any record until that time.[67]

Hazel's triumphs kept accumulating. The next three years saw her perform at Carnegie Hall, record a second album, and perform in a Broadway show called *Priorities of 1942*. Even as these opportunities came her way, Hazel had not forgotten her goal of changing conditions for African Americans in the United States. She began to require that the audiences at her performances be integrated. If she showed up at a concert or nightclub and the audience was segregated, she would walk out without playing. Not only would she not play, she would insist on being paid as well.[68]

By the summer of 1942, even though the United States was preoccupied with its entry into World War II, word of her popularity and skill had reached the West Coast, and Hollywood was interested in using her in films. Hazel knew that Hollywood studios treated black actors and actresses with disrespect and that they gave black women roles in which they were required to play mammies, maids, or prostitutes. She and her agent negotiated several clauses that would maintain her dignity in the roles she would accept. First, Hazel would have final approval of all of her musical numbers in a film. Then, if she thought that her wardrobe was unbecoming, she would wear her own gowns, furs, and jewels. Best of all, she would not be billed in the film with a character's name. The film credits would always say, "Hazel Scott as herself."[69]

With the details hammered out, Hazel signed a contract with RKO Pictures. Her first film was called *Something to Shout About*. In the film, Hazel's character is introduced as "the best pianist in the business." Just as her contract allowed, she rejected a song titled "You'd Be So Nice To Come Home To" by the famed Cole Porter. She said to the songwriter, "I just don't feel it." The song was nominated for an Academy Award and became a big hit. Hazel said years later, "The funny thing is, I *still* don't feel it! The idea of some guy lolling around the house waiting for *me* to come back from a hard day's work is singularly unattractive." Hazel always worked hard and would have wanted the love of her life to do the same.[70]

In her next film, *I Dood It*, Hazel appeared with someone she had met years before at an audition in New York City when Hazel was thirteen years old. Lena Horne was just as concerned as Hazel was with the way black women were portrayed in movies, and they became great friends. "Until the powers that be at M.G.M. stood Lena Horne up against a white pillar in *As Thousands Cheer*, as far as Hollywood was concerned, the women of our race were a bunch of dogs," Hazel wrote. "There had been one or two exceptions, but on the whole, we were relegated to the kitchen or the back stairs."[71] Hazel Scott and Lena Horne brought crowds of people into the movie theater, and critics loved them.

With such popularity, it is not surprising that Hazel and Lena appeared together in Hazel's next film, *The Heat's On*. Hazel had some memorable scenes, including one in which she played two grand pianos at the same time. The scene that would change her film career, however, was the final scene of the film. In that scene, Hazel played the piano while a group of African-American women danced with their boyfriends and husbands.

The day this part of the movie began filming, the director was sick and away from the movie set. The choreographer was setting up the costumes and directed his staff to put aprons on the women and make the aprons dirty, as if the women had just stepped out of the kitchen. Hazel objected. She knew that these women would never leave the house in dirty aprons to send their men off to war. Hazel and the choreographer ended up shouting at each other. Hazel refused to shoot the scene and went on strike.[72]

When the head of the movie studio, Harry Cohn, heard that a strike was happening and that the delay was costing thousands of dollars, he stepped in. Though he had admired Hazel, calling her "the most unusual girl (I have) ever seen," her strike was not something he approved of. [73] When he and Hazel met about the situation, she knew things would not turn out well for her. She wrote, "It was useless to attempt an explanation. It was impossible for me to declare my racial pride. All he could see was what he considered my treachery. I was costing him money."[74]

Harry Cohn would retaliate with a statement that changed her career: "She will never set foot in another movie studio as long as I live."[75]

The scene with the women and soldiers was shot with lovely dresses, and Hazel finished her work on the film. She also finished out her contract for the studio with two movies—*Broadway Rhythm* and *Rhapsody in Blue*—and left Hollywood.

"It's not that I object to having had to give up my Hollywood career," Hazel wrote. "The loss of my burgeoning career was a small price to pay for my self-respect."[76] She was proud of the professional standard of her work in films. Her popularity was riding high, and she had plenty of radio shows, concert dates, and performances in Las Vegas where she was one of the first black women to appear.[77] Before long, she would become part of the most famous, most photographed, and most universally followed African-American couple of her day.

7 / Service, Politics, Love, and Marriage

After the United States joined World War II, the film *The Heat's On* was one of many films Hollywood made to raise the morale of soldiers, their sweethearts, and all Americans. Artists and musicians donated their time to encourage and support these men and women who served their country. The music industry also made V-discs, which were records of popular songs to send to American troops overseas. The "V" stood for "Victory," a reminder that everyone back home was thinking of them and cheering them on.

Hazel did more than record songs for the soldiers. She also recorded film clips in her beautiful dresses, with diamonds sparkling in the lights, for *The Army / Navy Screen Magazine.* She played and sang at a club for soldiers called the Stage Door Canteen when she was in New York City, and she also performed in hospitals. She would even enter wards filled with servicemen with contagious diseases, and she would wear a mask and carry a portable piano with her. She was included in a radio broadcast called "Salute to Freedom" that honored African-American servicemen and women, and she also helped raise money for the war effort by selling war bonds. She answered thousands of letters from soldiers who loved her performances and sent out autographed photos to many more soldiers abroad.[78] At one point, she even sang for Russian soldiers who were allies of the United States at the time.[79] The branches of the military services thanked her with citations, and the Treasury Department was grateful for her fundraising.[80]

Being back in New York gave her time to be with her mother again. They still had an apartment in the city, but Hazel had bought a home north of Manhattan in White Plains where Alma lived now. Hazel knew Alma would be happy away from the city where she could grow vegetables in a victory garden and could spend her days as she wished, including quietly playing piano, while Hazel was busy elsewhere with her career.

Hazel was as popular as ever at Café Society, and fans crowded the club to hear her swing the classics. One reviewer from *Newsweek* wrote, "When she closes her eyes and looks enraptured as she plays the Chopin Waltz in C Sharp Minor as it was written, the audience looks impressed and enraptured too. When Hazel sighs, says 'Ah, yeah,' softly to herself and begins a beat which would bounce Chopin right out of his grave, her public grins and starts tapping the table."[81]

One of her fans who showed up often to hear her was an African-American minister in Harlem who was just beginning a political career. His name was Adam Clayton Powell, Jr. He described what it was like to see Hazel start her performance at the club: "At the end of the long room was the black concert grand piano sticking its nose up out of the audience. All the lights would go out, Hazel would make her way to the piano, and suddenly a spotlight would catch her. For a moment the audience would gasp . . . the height of the piano, the bare-shouldered dress, nothing but the golden brown shoulders and arms, the supertalented fingers."[82]

Adam and Hazel had originally met in Harlem. They both had been part of war rallies to support black soldiers who were on their way to the battlefront. Hazel remembered, "The first time I heard Adam Clayton Powell, Jr. exhort a crowd I tingled from head to toe and realized that I was in the presence of greatness."[83] Neither one held back when insisting on rights for black people. While Hazel headed to Hollywood to work in films and insist on a fair contract for black singers and actors, Adam helped the people of Harlem by marching in picket lines and speaking up for the oppressed.

The Abyssinian Baptist Church where he preached ran programs to help African Americans who were unemployed, as well as children who were suffering from malnutrition—whether they were in his church congregation or not. He organized a protest movement, which caught on in Chicago and Detroit as well as New York—to gain more employment for black people. The slogan was "Don't Buy Where You Can't Work!"[84] After the picketers closed stores down with their protests, the management was willing to negotiate with the minister and sign contracts to employ black people.

As a result of his efforts, Adam became the first African American to be elected to the New York City Council.

Adam's eyes were on Washington, D.C., however, and he began to campaign to be elected to the House of Representatives. His district included his most enthusiastic supporters, the residents of Harlem. He said, "I must run for the Congress of the United States, so that we may have a national voice speaking from the national capital. It doesn't matter what ticket or what party—my people demand a forthright, militant, anti-Uncle Tom Congressman! My cry today and until I die is let my people go—NOW!"[85]

Adam Clayton Powell, Jr. had fallen in love with Hazel Scott. However, there was an obstacle in the way of their becoming husband and wife: Adam was already married. Hazel turned to her mother for advice, who told her, "We don't run in this family. Either you're going to see Mr. Powell face to face and say to him, 'Sir I am not interested' or 'I am interested' or whatever it is that you are . . . or you are no daughter of mine."[86]

Hazel was interested, and Adam began the process of getting a divorce. Meanwhile, Hazel accompanied Adam to events big and small. She watched from the gallery as he was sworn in as a member of the Seventy-ninth Congress. She was very proud of Adam's dedication to the residents of his district who had elected him to office. Adam would walk through Harlem and shout to people on the street and from the pulpit, "Keep the Faith, Baby!"[87] He was always encouraging black people to have hope, and he worked hard to gain advantages for his people and for all who were poor and oppressed in the United States.

On August 1, 1945, Hazel and Adam were married. It was a quiet wedding, but the reception was held at Café Society with two thousand invited guests, and another thousand people showed up. Twenty-five police officers were needed to control the crowd outside the club, as they were all waiting to catch a glimpse of the bride and groom. Inside, music was playing, and actors, musicians, comedians, and politicians were trying to talk over the music. A two-foot-tall wedding cake was waiting for those who could reach it to get a piece. *Life* magazine published a shot of the couple soon after the wedding, and journalist Mike Wallace proclaimed, "They were stars, not only in the black world but the white world. That was extraordinary."[88]

It *was* extraordinary for an African-American couple to garner so much attention in the year 1945. The nationwide

movement for civil rights supporting the
equality of all people had not yet begun,
and most white Americans were not interested in reading about black people in
newspapers or magazines. However, the
press loved Adam and Hazel and would
follow them for years to print every photo

and publish every detail—whether real or invented—about these two remarkable people. Any news about Adam Clayton Powell, Jr. and Hazel Scott always sold very well.

8 / Dealing with Big Changes and Jim Crow

Now that they were married, Adam began to talk with Hazel about her work in nightclubs. He felt that a minister's wife should not be associated with places where people were drinking and smoking and where high moral standards were not part of the nightly scene. Since they had gotten to know each other while Hazel played the piano and sang in a nightclub, Hazel thought it was hypocritical of him to make this suggestion.[89]

It was especially hard for Hazel to give up her work at Café Society because it was the place where she had become a star. The job was a dream come true for her— the club was located close to her home, and it had regular hours and dependable pay.[90] This new restriction meant that she would also be giving up engagements in Las Vegas that paid her very well. In those performances, she would break the color barrier by appearing in casinos.[91]

Still, she knew what this change meant to Adam's congregation and to his future in politics. The wife of such a man could support him best by being dignified in the public eye, so she agreed to stop performing at both nightclubs and casinos.[92]

Hazel was now being booked for concert performances in big cities other than New York. Though she would be welcomed by fans and would successfully fill concert halls, touring was always especially hard on black performers. They could never be sure that they would find acceptable hotels and restaurants where they would be welcome to stay overnight and be able to eat. Laws that permitted discrimination against black people, called Jim Crow laws, existed in many states.[93] Hazel's agents had removed the clause in her contract that insisted that she only play in places where black and white people were equally welcome. They were thinking that they would only book her in concert halls where integration was practiced.[94]

Her agents did not always get it right, however. Upon arriving in Austin for one performance, Hazel saw that the hall was segregated. A red carpet down the center aisle separated the audience by skin color. She commented at the time, "Why would anyone come to hear me, a Negro, and refuse to sit next to someone like me?"[95] Hazel refused to perform and was escorted out of Austin by police officers called Texas Rangers.[96]

Being on the road was physically and emotionally exhausting for Hazel, both because of extended days of travel and because of the racist attitudes she dealt with on a daily basis. She faced this stress in both southern and northern states. On one trip to Spokane, Washington, Hazel's train was stuck in a snowdrift for three days. When a bus came to take the passengers into town where they could get some food, the waitress at the diner refused to serve her. Hazel found her way to the police station and prepared to lodge a complaint, but the desk sergeant said to her, "Are you going to get out of here or am I going to have to run you in for disturbing the police?"[97]

When Hazel phoned Adam back home, they decided to file a $50,000 lawsuit against the people who owned the diner. At the trial, the waitress, Hilma Victor, said that Hazel's behavior, rather than her race, was the reason she would not serve her, and she claimed that Hazel had been "sarcastic, haughty, and demanding."[98] Then a surprise witness came forward and said that Hazel, contrary to Hilma's testimony, "conducted herself in a lady-like manner and did not shout . . . use profanity, or threaten to tear apart the waitress."[99] After two days, the jury decided that the restaurant owners were at fault and fined them $250.00. Hazel was excited by this small victory for civil rights and immediately donated the money to the National Association for the Advancement of Colored People.

In the very heart of the country's government, Washington, D.C., Hazel was scheduled to perform in Constitution Hall. When the Daughters of the American Revolution, who oversaw programming there, found out about the performance, they refused to let her play. Some senators supported Adam and Hazel with statements against prejudice. One wrote, "It is indeed regrettable that such discriminatory action should be taken in the capital city of this nation which has just successfully concluded a long and costly war to stamp out a regime which was fostering just such intolerance in Europe . . . Racial discrimination has no place in this nation."[100]

Hazel was then invited to perform for the National Press Club's annual dinner, but Hazel discovered that African-American journalists were not allowed in the press galleries—which were controlled by that organization—of the Capitol Building. She canceled her appearance and said she could not perform for President Truman when black people were barred from the Capitol by the very group that was holding the dinner. Her husband, even though he was a member of the House of Representatives, was not even allowed to eat in the dining room that was reserved for members of Congress! Racism and Jim Crow laws—against which both she and her husband continued to fight—were certainly alive and well in the United States.

In the midst of traveling in 1945, other changes occurred in Hazel's life. First, the Second World War had ended in September of the same year, and the entire nation was celebrating. Even more exciting, in October, she discovered that she was pregnant. She and Adam were thrilled, and he announced to his congregation that "about June, there will be another big noise here beside me."[101] Then, an unexpected event caused Hazel's emotions to plunge. Alma, the mother whom Hazel adored, died of pneumonia a few days before Christmas.

She was only forty-six years old. Hazel was not certain she could continue traveling, performing, and recording without her mother's untiring love and support. For the rest of her life, she was quick to tell people that Alma Scott was "the biggest single influence in my life."[102]

In spite of the sorrow in her heart, the Christmas card that year—in Hazel's handwriting—read, "That the unity which won this war may win the peace; that this peace shall be one of good will between men of all races, nations and faiths—this be our heartfelt wish. Hazel and Adam Powell."[103]

9 / Excitement and Injustice

Adam Clayton Powell, III, nicknamed Skipper, was born on July 17, 1946. Motherhood was a wonderful experience for Hazel. "My greatest thrill was the first time I saw Skipper," said the woman who regularly rubbed shoulders with some of the most famous celebrities of her day.[104] Hazel was able to spend a total of six months with Skipper before her concert dates began to take her away from home. Though Hazel felt Alma's absence, the Powells had enough money to hire a lot of help. Adam had an equally busy schedule, but he made sure to be home with his son as often as possible.

Even though Hazel's career had changed with the cancellation of her steady night-

club act, she was as popular as ever in the late 1940s. She recorded two albums, then wrote an original suite titled *Caribbean Fete* and performed it to a full house at Carnegie Hall. Most remarkably, in 1950, she was offered a fifteen-minute television show, *The Hazel Scott Show*. She was the first black woman to have a show in which there were no other acts—no comedians and no roster of guests. She was the star host and performed solo.

The Hazel Scott Show was such a hit that the network extended it to air three times a week instead of once per week. Families across the United States tuned in to see the intelligent and talented woman play and sing. David Bogle, a film historian, wrote, "There sat the shimmering Scott at her piano, like an empress on her throne, presenting at every turn a vision of a woman of experience and sophistication."[105] On top of all of her other successes, she was proving to be a star on television as well as on the concert stage.

A few weeks after her television show began to air, Hazel's name appeared in a publication called *Red Channels*.[106] She was accused of being a Communist. A senator from Wisconsin named Joseph McCarthy helped instill into Americans the fear that Communists were trying to take over the government—and the whole country.[107]

Musicians, actors, and writers were one target of his accusations because many of them supported ideals that were seen as Communist ideals, such as the organization of unions for workers' rights and the right of equal opportunity for all people, regardless of their race or culture. Eventually, Senator McCarthy was proven wrong about his accusations, but not before Hazel was added to a do-not-hire list of people who he claimed were dangerous to the United States.

Ever since Hazel had been beaten up by a group of white boys in her own home as a five year old, she had learned to be strong and courageous, and fear was not part of her vocabulary. Stubbornness was one of her personality traits, but not cowardice. She said, "If I believe that I am in the right, I will die before I allow myself to be dissuaded. No one has ever been able to make me swerve from a decision once I have made up my mind. It has never been my practice to choose the popular course. When others lie as naturally as they breathe, I become frustrated and angry."[108]

Against the advice of all her friends, she volunteered to meet with HUAC, McCarthy's House (of Representatives) Un-American Activities Committee, which investigated accused Communists. She was determined to clear her name. After being grilled by committee members, she ended with these words: ". . . may I end with one request—and that is that your committee protect those Americans who have honestly, wholesomely, and unselfishly tried to perfect this country and make the guarantees in our Constitution live. The actors, musicians, artists, composers, and all of the men and women of the arts are eager and anxious to help, to serve. Our country needs us more today than ever before. We should not be written off by the vicious slanders of little and petty men."[109]

Raising her voice did not clear her name. Within one week of her testimony, *The Hazel Scott Show* was canceled. Hazel's career playing what she called her "Bach to Boogie-Woogie" repertoire began to slow down.[110] Concert performances became harder for her agents to book. Her insistence on playing for integrated audiences—along with her husband's insistence on her not playing in nightclubs—began to make it more difficult to find places to perform, and her sparkling stardom began to dim.

10 / A Very Public Life

Wherever the Powells went, the press followed them. Since performances were becoming sparse in the United States, Hazel decided to book a summer of concerts in Europe. Adam went with her and planned political appointments along the way, and they both showed Skipper the sights in London, Paris, and even various cities in the Middle East. It was difficult knowing that, no matter how anyone in the family was feeling, photographers were snapping away and capturing all the emotions—happy, angry, excited, tired—that the members of the Powell family showed in public. Hazel's patience for the necessary obligations to her fans was wearing thin. Toward the end of the summer together, Hazel said, "A person needs to go off somewhere and be alone so that his body can catch up with his soul. Before I got married, I did have some private life. But I find being a public figure and being married to a public figure makes privacy a luxury."[111]

Hazel and Adam, who had had plenty of ego clashes during their marriage, were finding it harder and harder to be together for long periods of time.[112] Because Adam

was regarded by his political opponents as someone who was seeking too much influence abroad, the family discovered that their hotel room in Paris was bugged by the FBI. Apparently, Adam had a very good rapport with many international leaders, and he was interested in the treatment African-American soldiers were receiving on military bases in other countries. Some of his colleagues considered Adam's concern for black soldiers to be a threat.[113]

It was all too much for Hazel. Even in private, the family was not alone. The pressure that had begun with her very public marriage to Congressman Powell was slowly building to a head. This burden had then been aggravated by her slowing career prospects, her mother's death, her increasing disagreements with Adam, and even her recurring memories of the stress of her childhood, when she had been a performer with family but had felt she had no real friends. The continual anxiety wore her down completely.[114]

One night, she was unable to go on stage for a performance. She went from anger to crying to numb silence, but nothing calmed her down. She was rushed to a hospital in Paris where she was diagnosed with a nervous breakdown. When she returned home, she fell into a deep depression. She began using alcohol and drugs to self-medicate, and at one point, she tried to take her own life.[115]

Adam managed to keep Hazel's breakdown out of the papers. After another hospitalization in the United States, Hazel slowly began to recover. Skipper, though only about six years old, was an important part of her returning health. She would play football with him and the kids in the neighborhood, go sailing, and do some of the things she loved most—cooking, gardening, and knitting. Skipper and Hazel often went out to dinner and charmed the guests who saw them together. Skipper would pull out Hazel's chair for her to sit down and would be the perfect gentleman.[116]

By the spring of 1952, Hazel was well enough to play at Carnegie Hall once again. She went to California to record with Capitol Records and made an album called *Hazel Scott's Late Show,* where she played songs by great American composers. She was feeling well enough to travel to Europe and to Haiti with Adam and Skipper.

Then Hazel traveled to Paris again, and while she was there, she felt she needed to stop drinking alcohol. She realized that whenever she drank, she turned into someone she did not like. She also longed to return to the religious tradition of the Catholic Church that she had practiced during her childhood in Trinidad. One day, she went to the great cathedral of Notre Dame. Adam reported that she "got down on her knees in front of the altar, and vowed she would not move until God gave her strength. She stayed there until her knees actually became bloody.

When she finally did rise to her feet, she had the power and strength of faith never again to touch or desire a drop of alcohol. She became an exceptionally religious person."[117]

11 / Endings and Beginnings

By 1955, Hazel knew that her marriage was not going to last. The pressure of publicity and both Adam's and her bigger-than-life personalities were tearing them apart. They denied their difficulties to the press but decided to live separately.[118] Hazel had spent several years visiting countries in Europe, where she had not only been a tourist with Adam and Skipper but had worked as well.

In 1957, she finally moved to Paris, where Skipper joined her. It was easier for her to work in Europe, where the cloud of the Communist accusations did not hang over her head. She began to perform in nightclubs again but was forced to settle for short engagements, unlike the long-term stability and sure income that she had known at Café Society. She was earning enough at the time to rent a luxurious apartment and to bring to Paris the gowns and jewels in which she performed, along with her "precious Steinway" piano that had been a gift from Adam.[119] By this time, she was far away from her husband and the judgement of his parishioners and political supporters.[120]

As the United States moved into a time when civil rights were in the spotlight, Hazel's hospitable home provided a place where friends and activists who were visiting from the United States could gather and enjoy each other's company. Hazel wrote, "My Paris is not the city of champagne and caviar. My Paris is a pot full of red beans and rice and an apartment full of old friends and glasses tinkling and the rich, happy sound of people laughing from the heart."[121] Similar to her mother's brownstone in Harlem, Hazel's home became a refuge for American artists of all kinds. Writer James Baldwin, bebop musician Dizzy Gillespie, and actor Anthony Quinn were just a few of the people who dropped in for good food and conversation.

Skipper, now eleven years old, loved the apartment where there were plenty of books and maps, a cat and a dog, and the beautiful, big Steinway that filled up most of the living room. He liked to lie underneath the piano whenever Hazel was playing so that he could listen to its vibrations.[122] Hazel reassured Skipper that his father would always be a part of their lives and told him, "Now, we're still going to be best friends. And I'll still yell at him on the phone."[123] Even though Skipper was surrounded by music and loved listening to it, he would eventually grow up to become a broadcast journalist and would work for CBS News, National Public Radio, and even as an executive producer for one of Hazel's friends—Quincy Jones—from these days in Paris.[124]

One last visit from Adam to her Paris apartment, with the aim of trying to bring them back together, started well. Much as he had when they first fell in love, Adam treated her with loving attention. He held her hands and gazed into her eyes whenever he spoke to her. Soon they were beginning to talk about having another child. But before long, the loving atmosphere evaporated, and Hazel came face to face with the old arguments and problems that had caused their initial separation. It became apparent to Hazel that being with Adam had been one cause of the "uncontrollable mood swings and violent outbursts" she had experienced when they had lived together.[125] Hazel fell into despair and tried to commit suicide again by taking an overdose of pills. This time, she almost succeeded. She was rushed to the hospital where she was listed as dead on arrival, but the doctors were eventually able to resuscitate her.[126]

When she had recovered enough to return to her apartment, her much-loved "sister," Billie Holliday, came to visit, along with other dear friends. Little by little, she returned to her true self and recovered her emotional equilibrium. She knew that she and Adam could not be together, but the love of her friends helped sustain her during this time. She wrote, "I learned a lot in Paris about people and about myself. One does not look into the face of death as I have and come away worrying about pettiness and cattiness and gossip and conforming. . . . The last time, when I spent a month or so in bed, I got the message. I am not likely to forget it. Love is important. Love."[127]

In 1958, Hazel was offered a part in a French film! She had always wanted to act again after her banishment from Hollywood, and here was her chance. The black-and-white film was called *Le Désordre et la Nuit* (The Disorder and the Night). She played a supporting role of a dancer, and she had to brush up on her French. As she arrived home from the first day of shooting, she saw a headline in the *New York Herald Tribune.* Harry Cohn, the man who had told her she would not work in film again while he was alive, had died. This became a favorite story of hers because she loved the drama of coincidence. She had outlived Harry Cohn and his curse on her acting career.[128]

A year later, in 1959, Hazel met a young Swiss-Italian comedian named Ezio Bedin. They were both performing at an open-air theater in Rome when he asked her to visit a nightclub with him. She accepted, and when their performances in Rome ended, Hazel gave him her address and phone number in Paris.[129]

Later, when Ezio visited, their friendship became a romance. He was fascinated by Hazel's sophistication and her many famous friends. They began to spend a lot of time together. Sometimes they traveled, and sometimes they performed at the same venue. Ezio finally moved in to the Paris apartment with Hazel and Skipper.[130]

After her divorce with Adam came through in 1960, Hazel and Ezio married. An interracial marriage was something the newspapers trumpeted, as such marriages were not an everyday occurrence in the 1950s and 60s in Europe. In an interview with *Jet* magazine, Hazel said, "It doesn't matter where we are as long as we're together. Of course, we aren't planning to settle in Mississippi or Alabama."[131] The couple bought a home in Manhattan, and although they periodically visited the United States for work, they maintained

Hazel's Paris apartment as well as a residence in Switzerland, and they would return to these places often.[132]

Maybe their age difference caused difficulties. Hazel was forty, and Ezio was twenty-five. Maybe Ezio was not quite ready for the role of stepfather as well as husband. Since Ezio had moved in with Hazel and her young son, Hazel began to realize that she had married quickly for Skipper's sake. Ezio often turned down opportunities to earn money in order to be with Hazel when she traveled to work. Over time, their income dwindled, and eventually, Ezio became tired of being known as "Mr. Scott." The relationship that began as a romance could not sustain the realities of everyday life, and by 1963, the couple had divorced.[133]

The year 1963 held more than a second broken marriage for Hazel. The civil rights movement in the United States was very much on her mind. Every time Martin Luther King, Jr. came to Europe, he stopped to see her. He would tell her, "Come on home, Hazel, because there's a whole generation of people growing up who are not being told of your contribution."[134] When Dr. King led the March on Washington in August of 1963, Hazel and her American friends living abroad planned a march in Paris in front of the American Embassy to coincide with it.

Along with her overwhelming concern for her fellow African Americans

back home, Hazel was dealing with severe financial difficulties in Paris. She was no longer earning salaries in the thousands, and she was barely able to make food and rent from month to month. Friends, including Dizzy Gillespie and his wife Lorraine, tried to help, but she was becoming destitute. Arriving home from a concert tour, she found her apartment filled with insects. The cupboards were empty, and the gas had been cut off because she could not afford to pay the bill. On top of these hardships, she suddenly became ill with mononucleosis and could not work at all. Somehow the press circulated the rumor that Hazel had leukemia, and her friends were eager to get her back home. Skipper, now a student at the Massachusetts Institute of Technology, wanted her to leave Paris and live near him again. She no longer tried to resist leaving Paris, and she returned to the United States in 1967. It was another unplanned, new beginning for her.[135]

12 / Hazel's Dream Job

Hazel was eager to contribute her reviving energy to the civil rights movement. Devastated by the assassinations of Dr. King and Malcolm X, as well as that of John Kennedy—who had supported civil rights—she was suddenly faced with accusations of having deserted her black brothers and sisters by leaving the country to live in Paris.[136] She faced these accusations with her usual strength and stubbornness. Addressing her accusers, she wrote, "When you were sitting very comfortable . . . I was down South deseg-regating audiences in town after town and getting out one jump ahead of the sheriff. So don't be telling me I ran away from the fight."[137] She especially encouraged the youth to take action to change the system and wrote, "Those who are for the right must take heart. There is no need to fal-ter. There is no place for self-doubt. There is no room for the slow to decide. There is not time for the dissension among the leadership—every clan must march."[138]

Along with her concentration on civil rights, Hazel was concerned that her career was slow to start up again in the United States. The music that was capturing the attention of the country at the time was folk, rock, and the tunes sung by British bands such as *The Beatles.* Jazz musicians were not in demand, and she had trouble finding the club dates that previously would simply have fallen into her lap.

Whenever people did show up to a club or concert to listen to her perform, however, they loved what they heard. She no longer relied heavily on jazzing up the classics but instead sang ballads and torch songs. She also played straight jazz and a little popular music. Occasionally, Art Tatum's "Tea for Two" would slip in, but Hazel had matured away from the swing sounds of her early days.[139]

There were a few opportunities for her to work in television, and in 1968, she appeared on the *Merv Griffin Show,* the *Mike Douglas Show,* and a show called *Girl Talk.*[140] After she had entertained passengers on a cruise ship, the *Queen Mary,* which docked in Los Angeles after its trip through the Panama Canal, Hazel landed roles in soap operas. She played a terminal cancer patient on *The Bold Ones: The New Doctors* and another character in two episodes of *One Life to Live.* She played Diahann Carroll's next-door neighbor in a series called *Julia.* Even in the 1960s and 70s, it was unusual for an African-American actress to be cast in television shows. Just as she had already done in the early 1940s, she continued to pave the way for decent roles for African-American actors and actresses of the future.[141]

Hazel had always embraced religion—all religion. She was interested in the ability of religion to lift people out of themselves and their everyday concerns to a place of love and acceptance for themselves and for others. While she was in California, Hazel reconnected with Dizzy Gillespie, who talked with her about his religion. It was not the first time she had heard about it, but this time, she wanted to become a part of it. On December 1, 1968, Hazel joined Dizzy in the religion he loved, and she became a member of the Bahá'í Faith. She said, "All my life people have said to me, 'The way you talk, you sound like a Bahá'í,' and I never knew what a Bahá'í was . . . I have always respected everyone's religion. As I say, there is only one God . . . That is what is great about Bahá'í; we believe in Progressive Revelation. We believe that whenever man has been ready to absorb more knowledge, God has revealed it."[142]

Hazel continued to shine as she aged. In 1975, she played again at Town Hall in Manhattan, the site of her first professional recital fifty years earlier. In 1978, she was inducted into the Black Filmmakers Hall of Fame, a nod to the mark she made in Hollywood on behalf of her people. From 1979 to 1980, she recorded three albums: *Always, Afterthoughts*, and *Afterhours*.[143]

However, her main occupation and the most important part of her later years was being a grandmother. She loved her grandchildren with her whole heart, and she gave her grandsons piano lessons and took them to movies. One of her grandchildren, Adam Clayton Powell IV, had this to say about Hazel: "She was a real person in her relationships, not being wrapped up in celebrity or anything else . . . Her family really came first. And we really felt and saw and experienced that."[144]

In the summer of 1981, she called Skipper with great excitement. She said, "I've got great news. This is fantastic news. *Your mother* has her dream job. Joe Kipnus is going to open a new room [for playing music in a restaurant] on 45th Street and he wants to name it after me. I can play as many weeks a year as I want. I don't have to be there all the time . . . I'll make more than enough money to live happily. And it will be a long-term deal. It will be years and years . . ."

Then she stopped.

Skipper asked, "What's the matter?"

And Hazel said, "Well you know the superstition. When you get your dream job, you're going to die."

Skipper laughed. He was not a person who took superstition seriously.[145]

During her first week at Kippy's, Hazel was so happy. She was getting good reviews, and she really could schedule her shows whenever it suited her. Then one night, she suddenly felt a wrenching pain in her stomach. She kept playing. After all, it was her room, and the crowd was loving the music. The pain kept getting worse, though, and she finally had to stop and rush to the hospital. Within a few hours, Hazel found out the news. She had pancreatic cancer.

Friends and family were drawn to Hazel's side to spend her last few weeks sharing funny and dramatic stories, but their time together was much too short. On October 2, 1981, Hazel Dorothy Scott died as her friend Dizzy Gillespie softly played his trumpet for her. The music that surrounded her, one of her favorite songs, was called "Alone Together."[146]

Hazel's funeral was held at the Abyssinian Baptist Church in Harlem where her first husband, and his father before him, had served as minister for so many years. It was a standing-room-only event with beautiful music that reflected the passing of such a skilled pianist. Musicians, artists, journalists, and politicians

crowded together to honor Hazel's life. Along with the rest of the program that day, they heard Adam Clayton Powel III read the words of Langston Hughes about this much-loved musician, his mother:

To Be Somebody

Little girl
Dreaming of a baby grand piano
(Not knowing there's a Steinway bigger, bigger)
Dreaming of a baby grand to play
That stretches paddle-tailed across the floor,
Not standing upright
Like a bad boy in the corner,
But sending music
Up the stairs and down the stairs

And out the door
To confound even Hazel Scott
Who might be passing.

Oh![147]

Hazel Scott was a strong, courageous, talented woman. She was wronged by the racism that even today infects the minds and hearts of many Americans. She was wronged by Senator McCarthy and the hate and fear that he doggedly fanned into flame in the United States. She stood up to discrimination of all kinds, called it out, and refused to tolerate it, no matter the cost to her life and her career. "Any woman who has a great deal to offer the world is in trouble," she had said. "And if she's a black woman, she's in deep trouble."[148]

We hear you, Hazel Scott. Whether speaking up for the rights of all people, playing two pianos at one time, singing a soft ballad, or swinging into Scarlatti's Sonata in C Major, we hear you. May your words, your music, and your story live on.

Timeline

Important Events in the Life of
Hazel Scott

1920   Born on June 11 in Port of Spain, Trinidad.

1922   Baby brother, the last of seven children, is born and dies. Only Hazel survives to grow up.

1922   Plays a hymn on the piano by ear for the first time and begins to perform calypso melodies.

1924   Sails to New York on her fourth birthday and ends up living in Harlem with her Aunt Lilla and Uncle Sydney, her mother Alma, and her grandmother Margaret.

1925   Starts receiving piano lessons from her mother. First professional recital in Manhattan at age 5.

1928   Auditions at Juilliard at age 8 and is taken on as a student there by Dr. Oscar Wagner.

1930   Hazel's mother and grandmother buy their own brownstone in Harlem, and the three of them move in together.

1931	Attends an all-girl junior high school where she especially loves reading and learning languages.
1933	Becomes known as the "Child Wonder Pianist" and continues to give concerts arranged by her mother.
1934	Joins her mother's all-women band—Alma Long Scott's American Creolians—and plays trumpet and piano in the band.
1935	At age 15, has a solo performance at the Roseland Ballroom on a program with the famous Count Basie Orchestra. Wins a six-month contract to play and sing on radio station WOR, the Voice of New York, and is able to choose her own program.
1938	Cast in the Broadway musical *Sing Out the News*. Her solo, "Franklin D. Roosevelt Jones," brings her positive attention from the critics. While performing in the Yacht Club in New York City, she starts to jazz up the classics. She briefly performs her own boogie-woogie song, "A Swingy Serenade," in the Hazel Scott Band (also called Fourteen Men and a Girl).
1939	Performs at the World's Fair. First recording session. Is hired to write arrangements for the Coleman Hawkins' big band. Billie Holiday arranges for Hazel to replace her at the Café Society in Harlem.

1940	Records her first solo album for Decca records, *Swinging the Classics: Piano Solos in Swing Style with Drums*. It breaks recording industry sales that year and sells thousands of copies in the first few weeks.
1941	Opens the second half of Carnegie Hall Concert and performs several encores. Her contracts for many years specify that she will only play for integrated audiences.
1942	Records second solo album, which includes some of her own compositions. Appears in *Priorities of 1942*, a Broadway vaudeville revival, and receives excellent reviews. Begins her film career in Hollywood.
1943	Appears in films *Something to Shout About, I Dood It,* and *The Heat's On.*
1944	Appears in movie *Broadway Rhythm* and plays in a Las Vegas casino. She is one of the first black women to perform there.
1945	Finishes filming her last movie in Hollywood, *Rhapsody in Blue*. Marries Adam Clayton Powell, Jr., in Stamford, Connecticut on August 1. Hazel's mother dies of pneumonia in December at age forty-six. Hazel calls her the "biggest single influence in my life."

1946	New contract with Signature Records produces *Hazel Scott: A Piano Recital.* Hazel's son, Adam Clayton Powell, III, nicknamed "Skipper," is born on July 17.
1948	Records *Great Scott* with Columbia Records.
1949	Performs an original suite, *Caribbean Fete,* at Carnegie Hall.
1950	Hosts her own television show, a first for a black woman. On September 22, testifies before House Un-American Activities Committee. *The Hazel Scott Show* is quickly canceled because of unfounded accusations that she is a Communist.
1951	Records an album in Paris titled *Hazel Scott.* Concerts in Europe are a huge success, but in the autumn, she has a nervous breakdown.
1952	Performs at Carnegie Hall with the New York Philharmonic-Symphony Orchestra in an evening of Gershwin.
1953	Records *Hazel Scott's Late Show* with Capitol Records.
1955	Returns to the Catholic Church and gives up alcohol. Records *Relaxed Piano Moods* for Debut Records, one of her "most significant recordings as a jazz pianist."[149] Charles Mingus and Max Roach join her for the Hazel Scott Trio.

1956	Records *'Round Midnight,* "one of the most in-spiring performances of Hazel's recording career."[150]
1957	Moves to Paris, France. After a visit from her husband meant to reconcile differences in their marriage, she attempts suicide. She recovers, vowing never to try to take her life again.
1958	Wins small roles in French films. Records an album for Polydor Records, *Hazel Scott: Joue et Chante* (Hazel Scott Plays and Sings).
1959	Meets Ezio Bedin, a Swiss-Italian comedian.
1960	Divorces Adam Clayton Powell, Jr.
1961	Marries Ezio Bedin. Performs for events for John F. Kennedy's presidential campaign.
1963	Divorces Ezio Bedin. Performs at the Cannes Film Festival and for the *Merv Griffin Show.* Helps organize a march in Paris to support Dr. Martin Luther King's March on Washington.
1967	Falls ill with mononucleosis and returns to the United States from Paris.[151]
1968	Begins appearing on the *Merv Griffin Show, Mike Douglas Show,* and *Girl Talk.* Becomes a member of the Bahá'í Faith.
1975	Plays at Town Hall in Manhattan, fifty years after her first performance there as a child.

1978	Is inducted into the Black Filmmakers Hall of Fame.[152]
1979–80	Records *Always, Afterthoughts*, and *After Hours*.
1981	Dies at age 61 on October 2 while Dizzy Gillespie plays trumpet softly in her room.

Notes

1. Taylor, *Notes and Tones: Musician-to-Musician Interviews,* p. 265.
2. The Universal Negro Improvement Association and African Communities League, https://www.theunia-acl.com/index.php/history/black-cross-nurses.
3. Slavery.com Editors, "Slavery in America," https://www.history.com/topics/black-history/slavery#section_2; Van Leeuwen, "Marcus Garvey and the United Negro Improvement Association," http://nationalhumanitiescenter.org/tserve/twenty/tkeyinfo/garvey.htm.
4. Sheldon, "Brief History of Black Women in the Military," https://www.womensmemorial.org/history-of-black-women.
5. Van Leeuwen, "Marcus Garvey and the United Negro Improvement Association," http://nationalhumanitiescenter.org/tserve/twenty/tkeyinfo/garvey.htm.
6. Chilton, *Hazel Scott: The Pioneering Journey of a Jazz Pianist from Café Society to Hollywood to HUAC,* p. 61.

7. Trusselle, "Spotlight on: Trinidad and Tobago," https://www.myristica.co/post/spotlight-on-trinidad-tobago.

8. Chilton, *Hazel Scott: The Pioneering Journey of a Jazz Pianist from Café Society to Hollywood to HUAC*, p. 6.

9. Ibid., p. 6.

10. Taylor, *Notes and Tones: Musician to Musician Interviews*, p. 254.

11. Chilton, *Hazel Scott: The Pioneering Journey of a Jazz Pianist from Café Society to Hollywood to HUAC*, p. 5.

12. Ibid., p. 8.

13. Ibid., p. 9.

14. Ibid.

15. PBS Learning Media, "Harlem in the 1920s: The African Americans," https://indiana.pbslearningmedia.org/resource/mr13.socst.us.harlem1920s/harlem-in-the-1920s/.

16. Chilton, *Hazel Scott: The Pioneering Journey of a Jazz Pianist from Café Society to Hollywood to HUAC*, p. 11.

17. Ibid., p. 13.

18. Ibid., p. 13.

19. Ibid., p. 16.

20. Ibid., p. 19.

21. Ibid., pp. 19–20.

22. Ibid., p. 20.

23. Ibid., p. 21.

24. Ibid., p. 21.

25. Music Division of the Juilliard School, https://www.juilliard.edu/music.

26. Chilton, *Hazel Scott: The Pioneering Journey of a Jazz Pianist from Café Society to Hollywood to HUAC*, pp. 22–23.

27. Ibid., p. 23.

28. Ibid., p. 24.

29. Ibid., p. 25.

30. Ibid., p. 26.

31. Ibid., p. 29.

32. Ibid., pp. 30, 32.

33. Ibid., p. 36.

34. Ibid., p. 37.

35. Ibid., p. 42.

36. Ibid., p. 47.

37. Ibid., p. 33.

38. Ibid., p. 33.

39. Ibid., p. 39.

40. Ibid., p. 33.

41. Ibid., p. 39.

42. Ibid., p. 36.

43. Encyclopaedia Brittanica, "Count Basie," https://www.britannica.com/biography/Count-Basie.

44. Chilton, *Hazel Scott: The Pioneering Journey of a Jazz Pianist from Café Society to Hollywood to HUAC*, p. 41.

45. Goldberg, "Whatever Happened to Hazel Scott?" https://www.youtube.com/watch?v=o_WJ4PpxWaE.

46. Chilton, *Hazel Scott: The Pioneering Journey of a Jazz Pianist from Café Society to Hollywood to HUAC*, p. 41.

47. Ibid., pp. 41–42.

48. Ibid., pp. 43–44.

49. Ibid., p. 44.

50. Ibid., p. 44.

51. H. Brothers, Inc., https://www.dollartimes.com/ inflation/inflation.php?amount=100&year=1938.

52. Chilton, *Hazel Scott: The Pioneering Journey of a Jazz Pianist from Café Society to Hollywood to HUAC*, pp. 45–46.

53. Ibid., p. 46.

54. Scutts, "This Piano Prodigy Was the First African-American Woman to Host Her Own TV Show," https://time.com/4507850/hazel-scott/.

55. Chilton, *Hazel Scott: The Pioneering Journey of a Jazz Pianist from Café Society to Hollywood to HUAC*, pp. 46–47.

56. Ibid., p. 46.

57. Ibid., p. 48.

58. Ibid., p. 47.

59. Ibid., p. 59.

60. Ibid., p. 58.

61. Ibid., pp. 55, 58.

62. Ibid., p. 55.

63. Ibid., p. 57.

64. Ibid., p. 57.

65. H. Brothers, Inc., https://www.dollartimes.com/
    inflation/inflation.php?amount=1500&year=1939.

66. Chilton, *Hazel Scott: The Pioneering Journey of a Jazz
    Pianist from Café Society to Hollywood to HUAC*, p.
    60.

67. Ibid., p. 63.

68. Ibid., p. 64.

69. Ibid., p. 73.

70. Ibid., pp. 75–76.

71. Ibid., p. 78.

72. Ibid., p. 83.

73. Ibid., p. 74.

74. Ibid., p. 84.

75. Ibid., p. 85.

76. Ibid., p. 87.

77. Johnson, "To Be Somebody: Hazel Scott," *Night Lights*,
    https://indianapublicmedia.org/nightlights/to-be-
    somebody-hazel-scott.php.

78. Chilton, *Hazel Scott: The Pioneering Journey of a Jazz Pianist from Café Society to Hollywood to HUAC*, p. 88.
79. Ibid., p. 143.
80. Ibid., p. 88.
81. Ibid., p. 89.
82. Ibid., p. 97.
83. Ibid., p. 97.
84. Ibid., p. 95.
85. Ibid., pp. 101–2.
86. Ibid., p. 104.
87. Ibid., p. 105.
88. Ibid., p. 108.
89. Ibid., p. 114.
90. Ibid., pp. 114–15.
91. Ibid., p. 116.
92. Ibid., p. 114.
93. Ibid., p. 137.
94. Ibid., p. 118.
95. Ibid., p. 138.
96. Ibid., p. 138.
97. Ibid., p. 139.
98. Ibid., p. 139.
99. Ibid., p. 140.
100. Ibid., p. 122.

101. Ibid., p. 126.

102. Ibid., p. 126.

103. Ibid., p. 127.

104. Ibid., p. 130.

105. Ibid., p. 141.

106. Ibid., p. 143.

107. History.com Editors, https://www.history.com/topics/cold-war/joseph-mccarthy.

108. Chilton, *Hazel Scott: The Pioneering Journey of a Jazz Pianist from Café Society to Hollywood to HUAC*, p. 144.

109. Rinehart, "This Black Woman Was Once the Biggest Star in Jazz. Here's Why You Never Heard of Her," https://narratively.com/this-black-woman-was-once-the-biggest-star-in-jazz-heres-why-youve-never-heard-of-her/.

110. Chilton, *Hazel Scott: The Pioneering Journey of a Jazz Pianist from Café Society to Hollywood to HUAC*, p. 134.

111. Ibid., p. 156.

112. Ibid., p. 154.

113. Ibid., p. 156.

114. Ibid., p. 157.

115. Ibid., pp. 157–58.

116. Ibid., p. 159.

117. Ibid., p. 165.

118. Ibid., p. 163.

119. Ibid., p. 173.

120. Ibid., p. 174.

121. Ibid., p. 173.

122. Ibid., pp. 173–74.

123. Ibid., p. 174.

124. USC Annenberg, https://annenberg.usc.edu/faculty/adam-clayton-powell-iii.

125. Chilton, *Hazel Scott: The Pioneering Journey of a Jazz Pianist from Café Society to Hollywood to HUAC*, p. 176.

126. Ibid., p. 176.

127. Ibid., pp. 176–77.

128. Ibid., p. 178.

129. Ibid., p. 182.

130. Ibid., p. 182.

131. Ibid., p. 189.

132. Ibid., pp. 182, 189.

133. Ibid., pp. 192–93.

134. Taylor, *Notes and Tones: Musician-to-Musician Interviews*, pp. 259–60.

135. Chilton, *Hazel Scott: The Pioneering Journey of a Jazz Pianist from Café Society to Hollywood to HUAC*, pp. 195–202.

136. Ibid., p. 204.

137. Taylor, *Notes and Tones: Musician-to-Musician Interviews*, p. 259.

138. Chilton, *Hazel Scott: The Pioneering Journey of a Jazz Pianist from Café Society to Hollywood to HUAC*, p. 205.

139. Ibid., p. 209.

140. Ibid., p. 209.

141. Ibid., p. 211.

142. Taylor, *Notes and Tones: Musician-to-Musician Interviews*, pp. 257–58.

143. T., Alicia, "Hazel Scott Biography," https://www.imdb.com/name/nm0779220/bio?ref_=nm_ov_bio_sm.

144. Chilton, *Hazel Scott: The Pioneering Journey of a Jazz Pianist from Café Society to Hollywood to HUAC*, p. 221.

145. Ibid., pp. 224–25.

146. Ibid., p. 225.

147. Ibid., p. 227.

148. Ibid., p. 219.

149. Ibid., p. 167.

150. Ibid., p. 170.

151. Goldberg, "Whatever Happened to Hazel Scott?" https://www.youtube.com/watch?v=o_WJ4PpxWaE.

152. T., Alicia, https://www.imdb.com/name/nm0779220/
bio?ref_=nm_ov_bio_sm.

Music Played by Hazel Scott Available Online

Army / Navy Screen Magazine: Hazel Scott performs for a film reel sent to U.S. troops during World War II. "Hazel Scott, Jazz and Classical Pianist, Performs Liszt." https://www.youtube.com/watch?v=0G_RztlV2q8.

Art Tatum. "Tea for Two," which Hazel Scott often performed. https://www.youtube.com/watch?v=kACt0FM0Kf8.

"Black and White Are Beautiful – Hazel Scott on 2 Grand Pianos." https://www.youtube.com/watch?v=1HdnjTCMzpg.

"Great Piano of Hazel Scott." ("Taking a Chance on Love.") https://www.youtube.com/watch?v=ySQ8cA4a-f8.

Hazel Scott. "A Foggy Day." https://www.youtube.com/watch?v=DTtX7QVaQWk.

"Hazel Scott in the Army." (Caisson Number from the film *The Heat's On.*) https://www.youtube.com/watch?v=EIbGi-cr0CSc.

Bibliography

Chilton, Karen. *Hazel Scott: The Pioneering Journey of a Jazz Pianist from Café Society to Hollywood to HUAC.* Ann Arbor, Michigan: The University of Michigan Press, 2008.

Goldberg, Eve. "Whatever Happened to Hazel Scott?" 2016. https://www.youtube.com/watch?v=o_WJ4PpxWaE.

H. Brothers Inc. Dollar Times. "Calculate the value of $100 in 1938." https://www.dollartimes.com/inflation/inflation.php?amount=100&year=1938.

———. "Calculate the value of $1500 in 1939." https://www.dollartimes.com/inflation/inflation.php?amount=1500&year=1939.

History.com Editors. "Joseph McCarthy." https://www.history.com/topics/cold-war/joseph-mccarthy. 2009. Updated 2016.

Johnson, David. "To Be Somebody: Hazel Scott." *Night Life.* October 21, 2020. https://indianapublicmedia.org/nightlights/to-be-somebody-hazel-scott.php.

Rinehart, Lorissa. "This Black Woman Was Once the Biggest Star in Jazz. Here's Why You've Never Heard of Her." 2018. https://narratively.com/this-black-woman-was-once-the-biggest-star-in-jazz-heres-why-youve-never-heard-of-her/.

Scutts, Joanna. *TIME.* "This Piano Prodigy Was the First African-American Woman to Host Her Own TV Show." September 27, 2016. https://time.com/4507850/hazel-scott/.

Sheldon, Kathryn. "Brief History of Black Women in the Military." 2019. https://www.womensmemorial.org/history-of-black-women.

Slavery.com Editors. "Slavery in America." Updated November 23, 2020. https://www.history.com/topics/black-history/slavery#section_2.

T., Alicia. "IMDB Mini Biography: Hazel Scott." (No date). https://www.imdb.com/name/nm0779220/bio?ref_=nm_ov_bio_sm.

Taylor, Anthony. *Notes and Tones: Musician to Musician Interviews.* New York, New York: Da Capo Press, 1993.

The Universal Negro Improvement Association and African Communities League. https://www.theunia-acl.com/index.php/history/black-cross-nurses.

USC Annenberg School for Communication and Journalism. https://annenberg.usc.edu/faculty/adam-clayton-powell-iii.

Van Leeuwen, David. "Marcus Garvey and the Universal Negro Improvement Association." 2000. http://nationalhumanitiescenter.org/tserve/twenty/tkeyinfo/garvey.htm.